OCT 2012

Stark County District Library
www.StarkLibrary.org
330.452.0665

D0889787

DR. BOB'S
AMAZING WORLD OF
ANIMALS
GRIZZLY BEARS

By Ruth Owen

WINDMILL
BOOKS
New York

Published in 2012 by Windmill Books, An Imprint of Rosen Publishing
29 East 21st Street, New York, NY 10010

Copyright © 2012 Ruby Tuesday Books Ltd

Adaptations to North American edition © 2012 Windmill Books, An Imprint of Rosen Publishing

All rights reserved. No part of this book may be reproduced in any form without permission in writing from the publisher, except by a reviewer.

Editor for Ruby Tuesday Books Ltd: Mark J. Sachner
U.S. Editor: Sara Antill
Designer: Trudi Webb

Photo Credits: Cover, 1, 4–5, 7, 8–9, 10–11, 13, 14–15, 16–17, 18–19, 20, 23, 25, 26–27, 28–29, 30 © Shutterstock; 20–21 (main), 22 © FLPA.

Library of Congress Cataloging-in-Publication Data

Owen, Ruth, 1967–
 Grizzly bears / by Ruth Owen.
    p. cm. — (Dr. Bob's amazing world of animals)
 Includes index.
 ISBN 978-1-61533-551-0 (library binding) — ISBN 978-1-61533-562-6 (pbk.) —
 ISBN 978-1-61533-563-3 (6-pack)
 1. Grizzly bear—Juvenile literature. I. Title.
 QL737.C27O956 2012
 599.784—dc23

                    2011031088

Manufactured in the United States of America

CPSIA Compliance Information: Batch #RTW2102WM: For Further Information contact Windmill Books, New York, New York at 1-866-478-0556

Contents

The Grizzly Bear

Welcome to my amazing world of animals. Today, we are visiting forests and mountains to find out about grizzly bears.

Let's investigate...

Hank's
WOOF OF WISDOM!

Grizzly bears are actually a type of brown bear. Other types of brown bear include Alaskan brown bears and Kodiak bears.

Grizzly bear fur can be black, blackish brown, and even a pale cream color.

A grizzly bear's brown fur has white or pale brown tips. This is how the bears got their name. The word "grizzly" means "sprinkled with gray."

The Land of the Grizzly Bear

Grizzly bears live mostly in Alaska and western Canada.

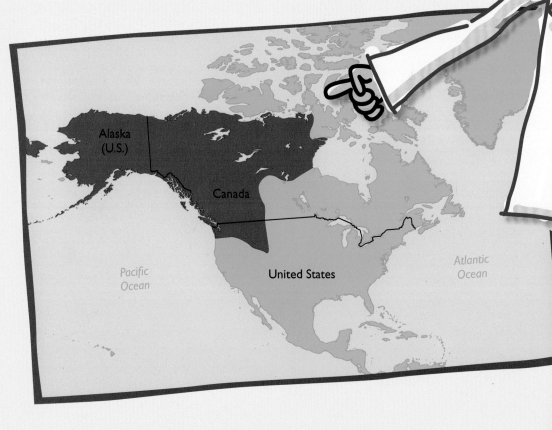

A small number of grizzly bears live in Idaho, Montana, Washington, and Wyoming.

Alaska (U.S.)

Canada

United States

Pacific Ocean

Atlantic Ocean

The areas colored in red on this map show where grizzly bears can be found.

Forest

Mountains

Grizzly bears live in many different **habitats**.

They live in thick forests and on open fields. Some live on mountains, and some live on areas of flat, cold **tundra**.

Hank's
WOOF OF WISDOM!

There are brown bears in parts of Europe, Asia, and the Middle East.

Grizzly Bear Bodies

A grizzly bear's fur is rough and thick during winter. In summer, grizzly bears may look patchy and scruffy as some of their fur falls out.

Grizzly bears often stand up on their back legs to look around for food or to check for danger.

A large grizzly bear may be 9 feet (2.7 m) tall when it stands on its back legs!

Grizzly Bear Size Chart

Weight (female) = up to 660 pounds (299 kg)

Height to shoulder = up to 4 feet (1.2 m)

Body length = up to 7 feet (2.1 m)

A grizzly bear can grow to over 9 feet (2.7 m) in length!

Weight (male) = Up to 1,500 pounds (680 kg)

What's on the Menu?

Grizzly bears are **omnivores**. This means they eat meat, fish, and plants.

Grizzly bears eat grasses and dig up plant roots. They eat berries, nuts, and insects, too.

Elk

Caribou

Young Moose

Sometimes grizzly bears hunt for deer, moose, elk, and caribou.

Grizzly bears also eat the dead bodies of animals. This food is known as **carrion**. Bears may cover carrion with grass and **moss** to keep it fresh. The moss contains chemicals that kill off any germs in the old meat.

Digging for Dinner

Grizzly bears have long claws. Each claw can be as long as a person's finger!

Grizzly bears use their claws to dig in soil to find insects. They also use them to pull apart logs to find tasty bugs.

Hank's **WOOF OF WISDOM!**

Grizzly bears spend winter sleeping in a home called a den. They use their long claws to dig the den.

These long claws are just right for holding onto big bones.

Gone Fishing!

Every year, grizzly bears get the chance to go fishing for delicious salmon!

When it is time for salmon to **mate**, they swim from the ocean back to the river where they were born. Sometimes they even leap up small waterfalls!

Small waterfall

Salmon

The hungry bears eat all the parts of the fish they can. Once they start to get full, they eat only the fishes' skin, brains, and eggs.

The bears wait in places where hundreds of salmon will pass by.

Getting Ready for Winter

In winter there is not enough food around to feed an adult grizzly bear. So, the bears go to sleep for the winter.

This long sleep is known as hibernation.

To get ready for **hibernation**, bears eat as much as they can in the summer and fall.

Hank's
WOOF OF WISDOM!

A bear may put on 3 pounds (1.4 kg) of weight a day to get ready for winter!

The bears build up lots of fat on their bodies. The fat feeds their bodies while they sleep.

17

Time to Sleep

As winter nears, a grizzly bear digs a big, cozy den. Then it is time to go to sleep.

The bear sleeps for up to six months. During this time, it does not even go to the bathroom!

Hank's **WOOF OF WISDOM!**

Brown bears that live in warm areas or in zoos in warm places often stay awake throughout the winter.

While the bear sleeps, its heartbeat slows down. It slows from 70 beats per minute to just 10 beats per minute.

Moms and Babies

Male and female grizzly bears get together to mate in early summer.

When winter comes, the female bear goes into her den to hibernate. In January or February, something amazing happens. While the female bear is sleeping, she gives birth to her babies, called cubs!

10-day-old cub

The tiny cubs have no fur and no teeth. Their eyes are tightly closed, and they cannot see yet.

A female may have one, two, three, or four cubs at one time.

Winter in the Den

The mother bear sleeps through the winter. The little cubs wrestle and play with each other.

The cubs drink milk from their mother.

They snuggle into her thick fur to keep warm.

When the cubs are about 6 weeks old, they open their eyes. Now the cubs can see! Their teeth and fur are growing, too!

Cubs drinking milk

In spring, the mother bear wakes up. It is time for the family to leave the den.

Time to Leave the Den

The grizzly bear family leaves the den when the cubs are about 4 months old.

The mother bear's body has been using her stores of fat all winter. She has also been making milk for her cubs. When she wakes up, the mother bear is very hungry. She may have lost one-third of her weight!

Bears need a little time to wake up fully from their hibernation.

The mother bear makes a comfy nest of grass and leaves outside the den. She sleeps in the sun, while the cubs play outside.

Protective Mother Bears

Some people think that grizzly bears will often attack humans. This isn't always true. Bears choose to stay away from people most of the time.

If a bear feels trapped, it may attack. Grizzly bears can run at speeds of 30 miles per hour (48 km/h)!

Mother grizzly bears are very protective of their cubs. People should never go near mothers and cubs.

If a mother bear feels her cubs are in danger, she will chase them up a tree.

Grizzly bear cubs stay with their mothers for 2 to 5 years.

The Future for Grizzly Bears

Grizzly bears once lived in many parts of North America. Today, outside of Alaska and Canada, there are fewer than 1,500 left!

People build towns and roads in the bears' habitat. They cut down forests for lumber. The bears have fewer places to live and find food.

Sometimes bears raid campsites or garbage cans to find food. Sometimes a hungry bear will kill a farmer's cow or sheep. People shoot the bears to stop them from coming near homes or farms.

Many people want to protect grizzly bears. A group called Defenders of Wildlife pays farmers money for cows or sheep killed by bears. This stops farmers from wanting to shoot the bears.

Glossary

carrion (KAR-ee-un)
The dead body of an animal that is starting to rot.

habitats (HA-buh-tats)
Places where animals or plants normally live. A habitat may be a rain forest, the ocean, or a backyard.

hibernation (hy-bur-NAY-shun)
Spending the winter in a sleeplike state, with heart rate and breathing rate slowed down.

mate (MAYT)
When a male and a female animal get together to produce young.

moss (MOS)
A small, low-growing plant that usually grows in cool, damp places such as forests. Lots of moss plants will grow close together and look like a green carpet.

omnivore (OM-nih-vor)
An animal that eats plants and also eats meat or fish, or both.

tundra (TUN-druh)
A frozen area with no trees and with black soil.

Dr. Bob's Fast Fact Board

Adult male bears are known as boars. Females are called sows.

When grizzly bears go salmon fishing, adult males get the best fishing spots. Females with cubs get the second-best places.

Grizzly bear cubs weigh less than 1.5 pounds (0.7 kg) when they are born. When the cubs leave the den, they weigh about 20 pounds (9 kg).

When their mother is in hibernation, grizzly bear cubs make a loud humming noise. This noise makes the mother bear's body produce milk for the cubs.

Web Sites

For Web resources related to the subject of this book, go to: **www.windmillbooks.com/weblinks** and select this book's title.

Read More

Kolpin, Molly. *Grizzly Bears*. Mankato, MN: Capstone Press, 2011.

Markle, Sandra. *Grizzly Bears*. Animal Predators. Minneapolis, MN: Lerner Publishing Group, 2009.

Sartore, Joel. *Face to Face with Grizzlies*. Face to Face with Animals. Des Moines, IA: National Geographic Children's Books, 2009.

Index

3 1333 04088 0013